THE LORDS OF MISRULE

JOHNS HOPKINS: POETRY AND FICTION

John T. Irwin, General Editor

the lords of

poems,

1992–2001

misrule

X. J. KENNEDY

The Johns Hopkins University Press Baltimore and London

This book has been brought to publication with the
generous assistance of the Albert Dowling Trust.

The Johns Hopkins University Press
2715 North Charles Street
Baltimore, Maryland 21218-4363
www.press.jhu.edu

Library of Congress Cataloging-in-Publication Data
Kennedy, X. J.
The lords of misrule : poems, 1992–2001 / X. J. Kennedy.
p. cm. — (Johns Hopkins, poetry and fiction)
ISBN 0-8018-7168-9 (pbk. : alk. paper)
I. Title. II. Series.
PS3521.E563 L67 2002
811'.54—dc21   2002069395

A catalog record for this book is available from the British Library.

FOR DOROTHY, AS EVER

Contents

THE LORDS OF MISRULE

Invocation

Bestriding hobbyhorses,
With cloth-headed dragons,
With sackbut and fife
Skipping and dancing,
The Lords of Misrule
Charge down the church aisle
One day past *All Hallows*
To launch celebration
Of the sacred birth.

They confine jubilation
To tolerable order,
Disperse fornicators
From the high altar,
Discourage the tippler
From toppling down drunk.

Come then, sweet Meter,
Come, strict-lipped Stanza,
Regulate the revels
Of these half-crocked lines.

1

"The Purpose of Time Is to Prevent Everything from Happening at Once"

Suppose your life a folded telescope
Durationless, collapsed in just a flash
As from your mother's womb you, bawling, drop
Into a nursing home. Suppose you crash
Your car, your marriage—toddler laying waste
A field of daisies, schoolkid, zit-faced teen
With lover zipping up your pants in haste
Hearing your parents' tread downstairs—all one.

Einstein was right. That would be too intense.
You need a chance to preen, to give a dull
Recital before an indifferent audience
Equally slow in jeering you and clapping.
Time takes its time unraveling. But, still,
You'll wonder when your life ends: Huh? What happened?

A Snapshot Rediscovered

for my cousin Mary

Your mother shrieked your name. We thought she'd die.
    You hadn't held stock-still—she'd snapped you throwing
    Your paper cup aloft, your panties showing,
Trapped in the old box camera's staring eye.

That watermelon kept cold in a stream
    Slid through our hands and shattered on the rocks,
    Yet here it is intact. The magic box
Whose simple click froze summer's passing dream

Has fastened you in childhood, long before
    You opened like a new-built house a life,
    That of a threadbare country doctor's wife.
How few the years till cancer closed your door.

But here you are with your invented toy,
    This empty cup suspended in midair,
    Arms lifted, sunlight drifting through your hair,
Your upturned face still wreathed in utter joy.

Jimmy Harlow

My third-best friend in grade school, Jimmy Harlow,
Like some shy twitch-nosed hare
Yearning to quit its burrow,
By teacher's harsh words once reduced to tears—
That day when, nine, you charged across the street
Not reckoning the car you'd meet by chance,
You stained a blanket thrown
To swerve the snowflakes from your broken bones.
You whined there, waiting for the ambulance.

After the accident
You lived just four more years,
Your skull crushed oblong, frail,
Face ashen-pale
And graven with an ineradicable squint.

I saw you last
At a New Year's party, locked in fierce embrace
With the loveliest girl in the place,
Dredging her with your sharp-chinned corpse-gray head.
I was aghast.
By April you were dead.

Lie in the ease of winter, Jimmy Harlow.
If I begrudged you her, I do not now.

Naomi Trimmer

Young, you aspired: a coloratura soprano
Whose blossoming solos might have been the rage
But for that moment on the concert stage
When fright struck. Hearing your cue repeat,
You croaked one raucous note, then turned and ran
In tears while your accompanist's piano
Pronounced a benediction on your slain
Career. A silence like a gale through wheat

Tore through the house. You straggled back home, mad,
To live alone. In bizarre homemade gowns
Of multicolored calico you'd flounce
Along our main street, curtsy to my dad,
Pee in the gutter daintily, demand
Your same seat at the dime-store lunch each noon,
Arriving not a second late or soon.
If someone had usurped your place, you'd stand

Muttering till he fled. Your room was cold,
You'd complain, shrilling, "I demand attention!"
Your janitor stood staring, mouth agape
At stacked sheet music luminous with mold,
Boas of fur, a mildewed opera cape—
He gazed with deepening incomprehension
Upon the relics of your long-closed show
And all your windows flung wide to the snow.

In memory you stride with lunatic smile,
Chin-chucks that triggered children's howls, immense
Frowsy rose-freighted hats, pink parasol,
Faint bows to an invisible audience,

Stalking our streets for decades till the blaze
Consumed your crumbling rooming house and caught
The fringes of your robe. And then our days
Grew colorless. A nuisance gone, some thought.

Five-and-Dime, Late Thirties

Your nose by frying franks'
    Salt pungent odor stung,
You'd perch on a stool, give thanks
    For shreds of turkey strung

On a mound of stuffing doled
    With ice-cream scoop, lone spoon
Of gray canned peas, one cold
    Roll, cranberry half-moon.

The same recorded air
    Swung round the counters daily:
Once more, "Old Rocking Chair"
    Recaptured Mildred Bailey.

Inclined, some lone gray head
    Off in a dream apart,
Selecting glasses, read
    With slow lips from a chart.

Nearby, a rouge-cheeked jade
    In permanent spit curls
Pushed Maybelline eyeshade
    To adolescent girls.

At times a beaten bell
    Insistent as Big Ben
Proclaimed the news: some swell
    Had tried to change a ten.

On to the thick cheap pads,
    Your last saved dime to blow,

To write fresh Iliads
    You'd steer course, even though

You longed for chocolates
    From the open-air glass case
Where, nightly, hordes of rats
    Shat in the licorice lace

Until one day the Board
    Of Health padlocked the door.
As sure as FDR
    Had kept us out of war,

Brown Shirts were just a show,
    Hitler a comic wraith
Far off. What you don't know
    Won't hurt had been our faith.

Sailors with the Clap

Slumped against bulkheads in the corridor
Beside the door to Sick Bay, they await
Their morning needle jabs and running-sore
Inspections, four who stayed ashore too late.
Deflecting with a bitter grin the taunts
Of passersby, each man smokes thoughtfully,
Counting his shots, those daily penances,
Like beads told on a cast-iron rosary.

Faithful as monks to rule, they to routine.
Dreading the engines' constant homeward drives,
Daily they pray, *Dear Lord, let not our wives*
Meet us until we once again come clean.
At sea, even Benedict or Alcuin
Might envy them their chastely ordered lives.

Deer Ticks

Adrift in the woods like mist,
She lifts slim breakable legs
Through fiddlehead ferns, stops, sniffs
The air for peril. Reassured, she strolls
With lethal hoofsteps, dropping stools,
Planting a rash called lyme.
Tick jaws clamp tight, as memory
Fastens on time.

Remember Eddie Brock, after he'd gone to
The Italian officers' brothel in Taranto
To try its famous sixteen-year-old whore
Who even let her patrons kiss her lips—
Shy as a fawn, they said, a girl next door—
Coughing up half his lungs
In the naval hospital's TB ward.

Who'd think a vision delicate as breeze
Could pack a sword?

Miss Olive Leahy's Rooms & Cigar Divan

Cork, 1956

Miss Olive had a couch where you could puff
   A cheap cigar before you went to bed.
Lights out at ten. You carefully placed your head,
   Avoiding where soiled feet had left their whiff.
The sheets—well, they'd be fresh on Friday nights,
   But it was Thursday. Dawn, and you adrift
In dream, compelled to rise, yield to the rights
   Of the next man, coming in from the night shift.

Breakfast? A cheap cigar, a cup of tay,
   And "Bless you, boys." That grim roof had been found
For us by the well-intentioned YMCA—
   In Cork, clandestine as Christ's underground.
Loose in the street, we ran into a dude
   In business suit who offered B & B
At his suburban house. He wheedled, wooed—
   Go-getter. Talked the last doubt out of me.

We went along with him. Americanly,
   His grass looked manicured, his frazzled wife
Patiently suffered each indignity.
   He made the poor wretch scurry for her life
And kicked the frightened kids out of their room,
   Consigned them to the basement. Feeling mean,
I slept uneasy in that furnished tomb.
   Miss Olive's, by comparison, seemed clean.

Salute Sweet Deceptions

Salute sweet deceptions:
At break of morning
How the brick firehouse
Seems carved from amber,

Beer cans in river
Mime stars dissolving,
A seed pearl necklace
Of rain wears phone wires.

For Allen Ginsberg

Ginsberg, Ginsberg, burning bright,
Taunter of the ultra right,
What blink of the Buddha's eye
Chose the day for you to die?

Queer pied piper, howling wild,
Mantra-minded flower child,
Queen of Maytime, misrule's lord,
Bawling, *Drop out! All aboard!*

Foe of fascist, bane of bomb,
Finger-cymbaled, chanting Om,
Proper poets' thorn in side,
Turner of a whole time's tide,

Who can fill your sloppy shoes?
What a catch for Death. We lose
Glee and sweetness, freaky light,
Ginsberg, Ginsberg, burning bright.

Visit

Through the expectant gates
You wheel, click radio off,
Stifle the noodling jazz,
Curve gradually up the drive
Of pebbles that rattle and sting,
Brake to a standstill, meet
There on the pillared porch
A woman with sun in her hands.

Faded silk gown, white hair,
She beckons you to drink
A pink thing in a glass.
"The birds are gone," she states,
"The house half boarded up
Against the growing cold."
And what of you?
        "Oh, I've
Outlived my day. And now
The children do not care.
They have no child themselves
To make the line go on.
I wait to be removed."

You scrutinize your drink.
Even her eyes withdraw.
You both fall still. The well
Is boarded up. The gods
Who once bestrode this house
Have gone upstairs to pack,
Their wings clipped, lips sewn shut,

Leaving this ruined estate
To wild, impersonal things—
The clover patch that snarls
With bees, the incessant grass.

Death of a First Child

in memory of M.J.G.

Christmas. The laden sack
    Draws noose-tight now its string,
The cherished gift sent back
    Though heralds sing,

Though tinkling carols drift
    And dull-tongued church bells toll,
An anti-gift is left
    Like stocking coal.

This year it seems not right
    To mouth old words of joy,
Bless the blind world, or light
    Candles without you, boy.

However brief, your fire
    Like a clear amber shone.
Your grieving dam and sire
    Shoulder a ton of stone.

I charge your spirit now:
    Although a searing blast
Of winter smote your bough,
    Be not the last

But one day harbinge in
    A further host, good son,
Of your deserving kin.
    Then you shall have begun

The raising of a house
  Beneath whose roof you fell.
In time your parents shall rejoice
  That in you they built well.

Epitaph Proposed
for the Headstone of S. R. Quiett

buried in the yard of the Primitive Baptist Church, Cade's Cove, Tennessee

Born with loud cries but carried off in quiet,
    I lie, the stillest of the Quiett boys.
Death sang a song so sweet I had to try it.
    I might have known. It's only empty noise.

Fat Cats in Egypt

The Homeless in Cairo Cemetery

> *Why should the dead have houses and we none?*
> These ghosts demand, alive and hollow eyed.
> Along the mausoleumed corridors
> They kindle campfires fed with dried bouquets,
> Ribboned brown wreaths. This wide necropolis
> Began as suburb, but the city grew
> And snarled it in a net of telephones.
> Westward in Giza, Cheops rears his tomb
> Proclaiming to the desert, *What I own*
> *Entitles me to heaven.* Latter-day
> Corpses of lesser wealth, whose names erode,
> Lie haunted by these outcast envious.

Thebes: In the Robber Village

> "They're lice!" declares our archeologist
> Turned tour guide, grinding out his cigarette.
> He steps on it with furious heel twist. "Why
> Aren't the scum rich? I'll tell you: every one
> Of them's an addict. Heroin comes high
> Because when caught a pusher has to die.
> Let's move. It's bloody hot here in the sun."

> He hates them for positioning mud huts
> Over mint tombs. By night they burrow down
> To scavenge golden combs and jars of coin,
> A hawk-beaked granite Horus, angry eyed,
> An alabaster Bes, that scowling dwarf,

Protector of the pregnant, a gold ring
That, held to light, reflects a heron's wing.
Winking at them with cameras, we stroll
Pursued by urchins. One thin barefoot girl
Nibbles from empty fingers. Given cash,
She yells—and we're surrounded in a flash
By babbling kids. A watchful tourist cop
Comes swooping down to stop
Our brief careers
As Francises and Clares,
Scatters the rabble, saves us and the day
With upthrust club. We make our getaway.

Our archeologist insists, in sore distress,
That henceforth we take vows of selfishness.

Mustafa Ferrari

In Edfu litter blithers on the wind
Down gritty streets. This mummy of a town
Asleep at noon, immobile as the Nile,
Surrounds the shrine of Horus, best preserved
Temple in all of Egypt, where, we're told,
At dawn the falcon-god will rearise.

We fat cats are to ride in convoy there,
Dragged by sick horses. Dutifully we queue
By twosomes for each surrey cloaked in black
To pull up and enhearse us. Here comes ours.
The dust parts to make way. It's something else—

A vehicle flamboyant, nonchalant,
Electric rainbows stenciled on its hull,
Numbered 2-0-0-1. A teenaged boy
Springs down to help us board. "American,
I am Mustafa Ferrari! I go fast!"
Tousled black hair, BULLS t-shirt. Merriment
Glints from his eyes. Deftly he swings aboard
And cracks his buggy whip. Away we lurch
Like a greased storm cloud down the mud-rut street.
"Come on, you sit up front!" Mustafa shouts—
I'll play his game. I climb up by his side—
"Is better to take picture." So I snap
A portrait of our horse's steaming ass.

I'm hanging on by one hand, ankle deep
In green hay, shell-shocked from the buckboard's jolt.
The whip keeps working. Briskly we arrive
At Horus's door. Mustafa shoves the reins
Into my hands, grabs camera, clicks a shot
Of horse and us. But when we clamber down
Our guide is red with outrage. He will ride
Shotgun on this kid upstart.

                              When we've paid
Our homage to the granite falcon-god,
The four of us depart. Slowly we clop
Back to the ship behind the humbled horse,
Mustafa getting hell in Arabic:
"You little rat! Why did you let that fool
Sit up in front? He fall and break his neck
And I'm in Dutch." Mustafa grins and shrugs—
"It wasn't me! What could I do? He asked

So he could take a picture."

　　　　　　　　　　　All the while
Mustafa casts me surreptitious grins.
I shrivel, chastened, in the safe back seat.
Farewell, Mustafa Ferrari. You have style.

Close Call

How suddenly she roused my ardor,
That woman with wide-open car door
Who, with a certain languid Sapphic
Grace into brisk rush-hour traffic
Stepped casually. I tromped the brake.
Her lips shaped softly, "My mistake."
Then for a moment as I glided
By, our glances coincided
And I drove off, whole rib cage filled
With joy at having not quite killed.

Street Moths

Mature enough to smoke but not to drink,
  Grown boys at night before the games arcade
Wearing tattoos that wash off in the sink
  Accelerate vain efforts to get laid.

Parading in formation past them, short
  Skirts and tight jeans pretending not to see
This pack of starving wolves who pay them court
  Turn noses up at cries of agony—

Baby, let's do it! Each suggestion falls
  Dead to the gutter to be swept aside
Like some presumptuous bug that hits brick walls,
  Rating a mere *Get lost* and death-ray eyes.

Still, they keep launching blundering campaigns,
  Trying their wings once more in hopeless flight:
Blind moths against the wires of window screens.
  Anything. Anything for a fix of light.

Others

The lurker in his jack-o'-lantern mask
    Soliciting small boys to sell him feels,
    Transvestites wobbling by on quaking heels,
The red-eyed bums who haunt dark parks to ask
Lone passersby of either sex for sex,
    Women who put their bodies up for bids
    Or, to retain their lovers, drown their kids,
The shooter-up who shotgun-slays his ex
For seeing other men—the record drips
    Carnage. Watching the nightly news scroll by,
    We say, There but for the grace of God go I,
As though their lives were our vicarious trips,
    But where we walk they loiter on the sly
And sometimes when we kiss we taste their lips.

Terminals

Bournes where no traveler ends,
Why do we call them terminals?
Overheated or cold.
Quit them as soon as possible.

People lip cupfuls of coffee,
Pour themselves stronger libations,
Get their hair cut, listen to clocks'
Automatic amputations.

Some people are bus waiting rooms
In whose custody time lags,
In whose houses bored children dispose
For no longer than need be, their bags.

In the Holding Lounge
at Frankfurt Airport

Here is a static island for the few
In transit who need help—the thickly veiled
Frail Pakistani woman of great age,
A human letter relatives have mailed,
And, solemn as a Puritan Sunday sermon,
The adultless American kid
Trying to read a comic book in German,
The wheelchaired invalid.

None heeds the offered checkerboard, toy blocks,
The never-ending clock's
Clickety lockstep. Each longs for a call
To a connecting flight. The feeble jokes
Attendants attempt don't fly. None accepts Cokes.
Tensely, all idle in sepulchral shade
While on dull walls distressed ad posters fade.

Karen! You come with me!
A girl of nine lifts chin
And breaks out in a grin.
For us, she's like beholding the full moon
Reflected in a tar pit,
A lost pearl turned up in a dusty room,
An apparition torn from earth caked hard:
The squash's delicate tissue paper bloom.

Police Court Saturday Morning

Hauled from their bunks in separate cells,
    The couples, bleary-eyed, in shock,
Enter a room where time stands still,
    Snipped by a brisk electric clock.

The drunks who last night beat their wives,
    The wives who tried to carve their mates
By cops disarmed of kitchen knives,
    Disheveled, face the magistrate's

Hard glare and sit without retort,
    Snuggled in solitudes, bereft
Of will to save themselves. Love's short
    And when it's gone what else is left.

Décor

This funky pizza parlor decks its walls
　　With family portraits some descendant junked:
Ornately framed, the scrap from dealers' hauls,
　　Their names and all who cared for them defunct.

These pallid ladies in strict corsets locked,
　　These gentlemen in yokes of celluloid—
What are they now? Mere human cuckoo clocks,
　　Fixed faces doomed to hang and look annoyed

While down they stare in helpless resignation
　　From painted backdrops—waterfalls and trees—
On blue-jeaned lovers making assignation
　　Over a pepperoni double cheese.

Covering the Massacre

Producers of the evening news
    Declare the corpses overdressed
And rearrange for close-up views
    The infant at its mother's breast,

Then bribe the rebel general
    Wrapped in his gun belt and vainglory
To suck up to the mike and tell
    His inside version of the story.

Head correspondent, popping pills,
    Comes roaring in on four-wheel drive
To the makeshift clinic, where he grills
    The only victim left alive.

With beaming face, a satellite
    Transmits a slim glimpse of the scene
Plus commentary—quick sound bite—
    To each far-off indifferent screen

Between the ads for dandruff cures
    And deals on high-performance cars
Where for a moment it obscures
    The stares of unforgiving stars.

narratives

The Ballad of Fenimore Woolson
and Henry James

Constance Fenimore Woolson,
Expatriate in middle years,
Had to tilt back her head to listen
Through the keener of her shell-pink ears.

Uncle Jim had created Leatherstocking,
But a true bluestocking was she
And her fiction of artist-heroines
Left her free to live fancy free.

Women writers, she knew, in retired shade grew
While the sun shone on male scribes' names;
Still, a glimmer of admiration grew
Between her and Henry James.

Now a diffident hat-tilt from Henry
Might fend off her loneliness,
But Henry was wedded already, it seemed,
To his ethical consciousness.

Down the twilit Strand, not quite hand in hand,
Folded handkerchiefs on their wrists,
They would sidestep drunks and Victorian punks
And the placards of anarchists.

On a steam train chugging to Stonehenge,
Inquired Fenimore, "Were you a druid,
Henry, would your granite dagger
Scatter my vital fluid?"

"Why," said Henry, "you obstinate pagan!
Do you crave such a sanguine feast?
I'd hardly know whom to sacrifice you to,
For an artist is his own high priest."

One evening as Fenimore went strolling
Near Hyde Park, rioting mobs
Of the hungry were halting the hansom cabs,
Planting kisses on duchesses' gobs.

Pale Fenimore's heart beat faster
To behold such an outrage occur.
She walked a while wistfully after the mob,
But nobody halted her.

In her villa in Florence, Henry
Came to stay under Fenimore's roof
Where he, although ever considerate,
Kept distinctly a bit aloof.

Wrote Fenimore, "Mr. James is coldish,
With a brown beard, taller than John Hay,
And a beautiful regular profile,
Large expressionless eyes, light gray.

"Mr. James would infiltrate me
With his own sense of the past.
He insists I admire the Duomo
But I find it too cold and vast.

"Insufficiently acquainted
With nude torsos, flanks, and the lot,
I can't tell the supremely beautiful
From bare bottoms that are not."

Oh, they'd drive their pens every morning,
Cappuccino for fuel. With sighs,
Each would labor upon a love scene.
A long lunch, and they'd revise.

The wily old cook who attended them
With brandy-breath and prescient leer
Brought Henry brief notes from Fenimore—
Gesù Cristo, quest'Inglèsi were queer!

Henry fled. He wrote back to Fenimore
Deft sentiments out of his heart
Signed "faithfully," which, as the weeks went by,
Grew noticeably farther apart.

Fenimore went to the Dolomite Alps,
Stared up at the masses of snow.
She stood in her chemise, only ten degrees
In her inn room. Where now to go?

In a palace in Venice, Fenimore
Fell ill with a feverish flu.
She turned and she tossed, knew all was lost,
And she knew what she needed to do.

Fenimore lurched to the casement,
Flung her left leg over the sill,
Crying, "Lord, if you're watching, forgive me,
But the sum of it all is nil.

"I shall join the eternal mountains,
Be an object of beauty, and then
Have no more to do with the sorrow
And despair of women and men."

Some passerby kicked at a bundle
Of white rags that uttered moans—
It was Fenimore leaking her life away
On the cold-nosed cobblestones.

Back in London, Henry at high tea
Accepted a wire with the word.
He added a spoonful of sugar to his cup
Though the first he had not yet stirred.

Henry walked down Great Ormond Street,
He lifted gaze to the air
And asked, "Tell me, my sensibility,
Was there aught of which I wasn't aware?"

But the air, uncomprehending,
Kept silent all the while
Although he had tendered his question
In his earlier lucid style.

Sifting Fenimore's papers, Henry
Came on letters in his own hand
Upon which with speed he set flames to feed
Lest anyone misunderstand.

Henry had a dream: he was running
Through a jungle in desperate haste
Where muffled footfalls drew near, drew near,
And the breath of an unseen beast.

In Rome, at the Protestant Cemetery,
Henry rang at the wrought iron gate,
Sent in his visiting card, ascertained
That his stickpin was stuck in straight.

"Who's there?" whispered Fenimore, rising,
"Who's making that dreadful din?"—
She took one glance at his visiting card
And sent word she wasn't in.

Henry kept standing and standing.
Why, there must be some hideous mistake.
Above him a lowering storm cloud
Relinquished a lonesome flake.

He slipped through the gate and beheld it:
The plot where she now dwelled apart,
Where a pride of stray cats came prowling
For a morsel of Shelley's heart,

Where the broth of the brawling empire
Seethed under its cloud-cover lid
And time had transformed to silver
The absurd old Pyramid

And her newly placed cross. He would fling him
Like a whipped dog across her grave!
Yet as he drew ready to do so
He knew that such a gesture would save.

Henry went back to his writing desk,
Spread paper like an open chart
And he drew dear Fenimore into his arms
And transformed her to a work of art
Still living,
Transformed her to a work of art.

Heard through the Walls
of the Racetrack Glen Motel

Where do you think you're going, kid?

                                          Out front

To get more ice. I can't drink lukewarm booze.
I'll be right back.

                Come here a minute, runt.
You ain't much, but you're all I got to lose.
Gimme a little kiss—how come the tie?
You going somewhere? What's the billfold for?
I thought they gave the ice cubes out for free.
Don't tell me you're fed up with me. I snore?

I said I loved you.

                That was in some bar.
You said it like you'd say "potato chip."
This afternoon let's buy us a sports car—
Red, like you go for, that'll give the slip
To anything but me.

                    Aw, May, Chrissake,
You bribe just like my mother.

                        Well I ought
To be her, maybe.

                  Pretty soon you'll make
Me drink my milk.

                Tease easy, kid. I'm caught
And twisting on the hook. I need you bad.
I seen too many like you disappear
To let you go.

            Don't tell me YOU been had.
I'll only be an hour or so.

                Stay here.

Afterward

Dazed, on each other's nakedness they stared,
The tang of fruit receding. Overhead
The hissing of an incandescent sword
Impelled them down the hillside. On they fled

To lands where brambles coiled as if to strike
And hornets swarmed. Night settling by degrees,
They drank pollution from a rotted brook.
Corruption gripped the fringes of the trees.

Circles of eyes that glowered from a wood
Of shapes about to leap seemed not unkind.
On berries that the birds had spared they fed.
The past roared like a bonfire in the mind.

Kneeling to rest beside a stagnant pool
Prinked by the evening star's myopic stare,
He touched his alien face. Within that still
Mirror a wreath of age moved through his hair,

Shadowed his brow. The bluster of the wind
Bore jackals' howls—he leaped up at a shout
From Woman, watching a firefly in her hand
Stiffen its wings and switch its daylight out.

The Blessing of the Bikes

The pastor of St. Daniel's Church in Lyncourt, N.Y., held his annual "blessing of the bikes" ceremony yesterday in the church parking lot. More than 400 motorcyclists attend the spring rite, which signifies the start of the riding season.   —*AP news item*

It's that morning of mornings in April
When the mockingbirds oil up and sing,
So I yank snakeskin pants on at dawning,
Head for church, engine going ka-jing.

There's suburbans with high-boughten karma
In their kangaroo-fur safety suits,
Even, revving a Ducati Darmah,
A couple of gray-headed coots;

There are Hell's Angels studded and goggled
Under helmets with steeple-top spikes—
All the bunch of us mounted and clinging
To those old rugged crosses, our bikes.

So I elbow my hog a bit closer
And Monsignor he solemnly takes
Up his sprinkler of blest holy water
And bestows us a couple of shakes,

Then he mutters some magic in Latin
Asking Jesus to pull a few wires
That'll keep us from sure-fire damnation
Should the treads ever peel off our tires.

So my pimple-faced skinny old lady
Jumps aboard, with her shuddering crotch
Crushed up next to my butt while I kick off
And ease up to speed notch by notch.

Well, we're off like a clean whoosh of whaleshit.
Oh, we're one nasty beast, one mean boat.
I wind open the throttle in second
And an anthem growls out of its throat.

Bitter road dust and rattle of pebbles,
Bugs we eat—nothing matters a damn,
For the spring air soars by, consecrated
By the blessing of I AM WHO I AM.

Superhuman, I peer through black plastic,
Passing Jags like they're nothing but wrecks,
For the Virgin is perched on my handlebars
Keeping watch on our breakable necks.

3 satires
and
versions

A Scandal in the Suburbs

We had to have him put away,
For what if he'd grown vicious?
To play faith healer, give away
Stale bread and stinking fishes!
His soapbox preaching set the tongues
Of all the neighbors going.
Odd stuff: how lilies never spin
And birds don't bother sowing.
Why, bums were coming to the door—
His pockets had no bottom—
And then—the foot wash from that whore!
We signed. They came and got him.

Pileup

Deep in our ranks a tire blew, and our pack
Stacked itself six-deep on our leader's back—
Then from the north, fresh skid marks counterscored
That abrupt mountain founded on one Ford,
A merge of metal half a mile across.
Cooling in seat belts, dazed in total loss,
We sat there all one long eight-nighted day,
Gridlocked, still beeping for our right of way.

It seemed that we'd elected to retreat
To distinct Trappist walls. The Paraclete
Bestrode the muddied water of our minds;
The stricken dark solidified its blinds.
A man who'd carried pigeons in a cote
Threw one aloft. It circled, grew remote,
Vanished. And then it came back in a week,
An olive-loaf-on-rye clutched in its beak.
Though time dragged on and some survivors kissed,
Life out beyond held little that we missed.
A man two wrecks ahead of me complained
That his crabgrass campaign had got behind,
A woman in a pickup truck gave birth.
A hobnailed wind kept gusting from the north.
Some frisked the scattered bodies. We did not.
The sky rained balanced dinners, piping hot,
On Red Cross parachutes. To fix the hinge
In someone's smashed leg in the outer fringe,
They coptered surgeons. Deep-voiced as the grave,
Our radios reiterated balm—
Your rescuers are nearing now! Keep calm—
While Lady Vanna from her limousine

Dispensed free condom packs and Vaseline.
We sat attentive in the thickening gloom
To spot commercials, burning to consume.

At last, across the dawn a copter crawled
Like a slow Mayfly. Amplifiers bawled:
Drivers, stand by—light's opening ahead.
A crew is on its way. Prepare your dead.
Tingeing the sky, the sweet acetylene
Kept carving, carving at the pileup. Clean
And freed at last, the road ahead lay clear
And, salvaged, off we roared in second gear.

Then and Now

I half long for those crappy days again
   When babies used to be produced by sex,
Back before women washed their hands of men
   And switched to being corporate execs.
Now, nearing forty, weary of their own
   Private Lear jets with uniformed wine tasters,
They tap the sperm bank for a little loan,
   Inseminate themselves with turkey basters.

Those were the days of pumpkin pie and dads
   Rigging kids kites, grim days before divorce,
Of home-brought bacon, nights out with the lads,
     And moose heads goggling from the mortgaged walls.
   God was no vaguely feminine Life Force
    But Old Pop Yahweh, hung with beard and balls.

Commuter

Rosary rattling at my steering wheel,
I do six decades battling through the squeal
Of brake drums inching home on Storrow Drive.
Saint Christopher, who brings us back alive,
You rate a candle—damn that Caddie's ass.
Our Father who—green light, give her the gas,
Nose out that biddy's Nissan. Him that prays,
He makes out like a bandit lots of ways.
Hail Mary, full of grace—a person needs
For luck a daily lap around the beads.
Why, every time some subway-begging nun
Asks for a quarter, hell, I give her one,
And sure as shooting, when the whooping cough
Almost took little Patty, faith paid off.
I pitched the missions five bucks and two jacks
Came back from car inspection. Excise tax
Skipped me entirely. Mother Mary, dear,
Put a good word for me in your Son's ear.
Our shrine works fine except for one bum part,
We've burnt a bulb out in our Sacred Heart.

Mr. Longfellow's Iron Pen

The pen was made of a bit of iron from the prison of Bonnivard at Chillon;
the handle of wood from the Frigate Constitution; and bound with a circlet
of gold, inset with three precious stones from Siberia, Ceylon, and Maine.
It was a gift from Miss Helen Hamlin, of Bangor, Maine.

—H.W. Longfellow's note to his poem "The Iron Pen"

He clutched his gift, but felt it sink
Under its freight of iron and ink.
No syllable bestrode his brain
But tripped flat on its ankle chain,

And rattling in his fancy's hold
Shackles of fourteen-carat gold,
One line kept bawling through its grate:
Thou too sail on, O ship of state!

With gentle curse he let his stare
Divagate through the twilit air
Where, level with the sunset still,
The wandering Charles pursued her will.

Siberia, Ceylon, and Maine
Rattled their stones. He grasped in vain
For words that scattered, let them go
And wrote with a pencil stamped *Thoreau.*

Obscenity

An epistle to Keith Waldrop

Now round about, taste wheels
    And saner voices still
The pack that dogged the heels
    Of honest Fanny Hill,

That once dived to impound
    At the sea trunk's bottom layer
Tropic of Cancer bound
    As *Book of Common Prayer.*

High time. But though one war
    Is done with, strange to tell,
In disarray lies more
    Than Comstock's citadel:

In prudery's aftermath
    Come harvesters newborn
Strewing a golden path
    With bundles made from porn.

While *Virgin Lusts* unreel
    Dim throngs of the devout
In darkened temples kneel
    To let it all hang out

Like drying pantyhose.
    Penthouse's monthly fix
Comes cut with airy prose
    On art and politics.

Now discount pharmacies
    Display on every side
Romanticized new ways
    To commit spermicide.

While on the Internet,
    Of viruses afraid,
Some men prefer to get
    Vicariously laid,

Play games by CD-ROM
    And, to help dreams congeal,
Delve a fictitious womb
    That's virtually real.

Can actual love endure?
    In videos we find
Sex technique stripped so bare
    It bares mere abstract mind:

When orgasm rehearsed
    Becomes a dial to twist
Old Puritan reversed
    Turns new sex therapist.

Each gender acts as if
    It were grim toil to mesh,
Seated intent and stiff
    On straight-backed chairs of flesh;

Then, all desiring done,
   Rest fallen on tired thighs,
What can each do alone
   But reconceptualize?

What can they know of love
   That scorches till it hurt
Wholehearted soul? What of
   Clean Rabelaisian dirt?

No Oyster Nan who heaves
   Her thighs like sloshing tubs
Turns bored executives
   To swine in lap-dance clubs.

No website though it tease,
   No film with core steel-hard
Can blaze like Eloise
   For kindly Abelard.

Arf! arf! the smut hound bays,
   Belaboring his flea.
True lovers let us praise
   And pure indecency.

Ballade of the Hanged

after François Villon

Brothers of flesh and blood, who shall outlive
The likes of us poor bastards, do not spurn
Our pleas with hard hearts. Pity us, forgive,
That God may grant you mercy in your turn.
Behold us dangling here: six slow to learn
Whose bellies rot, once fat and overfed,
Now served to crows that banquet on the dead,
Ashes and dust the skulls inside our skins.
Let no man snicker at the lives we've led
But pray the Lord to shrive us of our sins.

If you would be our brothers, don't disdain
Us just because we ended on a rope.
Not everyone is born with equal brain.
We pray you, do not play the misanthrope.
Pity us, banished from this world of late
To stand before the Virgin Mary's Son.
Pray that His mercy shan't evaporate
But rescue us ere Hell's meltdown begin.
Now that we're dead, what man can give us pain?
Dear Lord and Savior, shrive our souls of sin.

Laundered by rain, by winter lashed and blown,
Charred black by summer, by the sun scorched dry,
We've let the ravens excavate each eye,
Pluck beards and pubic hair down to bare bone.
Hither and thither as the wind decrees,
Restless we drift. We can no more bend knees
Nor sit again. Each vacuous corpse spins,

Poked by more beaks than seamstresses have pins.
Count not yourselves with our tormenters, please,
But pray the Lord to shrive us of our sins.

Prince Jesus, ruler of the skies and seas,
Spare us Hell's vats of incandescent grease.
No gambler with the Devil ever wins.
Men, do not mock us. Pray we find surcease
And pray the Lord to shrive us of our sins.

The Spoke

after Salvatore Quasimodo

All alone
On the earth's heart
Stands everyone
Impaled
Upon the sun's last spoke of light.

And quicker than he knows
It's night.

4

A Beard of Bees

at the farmers' market

The arbor of his chin
Bedangled with a cluster
Of yellow grapes that buzz
Like an electric razor,
This raiser of honeybees
With face in half-eclipse
Coaxes some hairs aside
To clear space for his lips.

He's a master of close shaves.
How well he does one thing,
With what abandon braves
Disaster's sting
Quite unlike refugees
Crossing a land mine sector.
A whir—his mustache flies
Away in search of nectar.

A Curse on a Thief

Paul Dempster had a handsome tackle box
In which he'd stored up gems for twenty years:
Hooks marvelously sharp, ingenious lures
Jointed to look alive. He went to Fox

Lake, placed it on his dock, went in and poured
Himself a frosty Coors, returned to find
Some craven sneak had stolen in behind
His back and crooked his entire treasure horde.

Bad cess upon the bastard! May the bass
He catches with Paul Dempster's pilfered gear
Jump from his creel, make haste for his bare rear,
And, fins outthrust, slide up his underpass.

May each ill-gotten catfish in his pan
Sizzle his lips and peel away the skin.
May every perch his pilfered lines reel in
Oblige him to spend decades on the can.

May he be made to munch a pickerel raw,
Its steely gaze fixed on him as he chews,
Choking on every bite, while metal screws
Inexorably lock his lower jaw,

And having eaten, may he be transformed
Into a trout himself, with gills and scales,
A stupid gasper that a hook impales,
In Hell's hot griddle may he be well warmed

And served with shots of lava on the rocks
To shrieking imps indifferent to his moans
Who'll rend his flesh and pick apart his bones,
Poor fish who hooked Paul Dempster's tackle box.

On Song

How odd that verse that's song
Should so displease the young.
They are so serious.
They hate all artifice
As standing in the way
Of mind's insistent say.

But to my mind what counts
Is language that surmounts
The message it must bear,
Steps back without a care
And, stone blind, yields the day
To bloodstream's reckless play.

Taking Aspirin

Go, boats of the blood,
Carry your cargo of ease to the ports of the body,
Unload surcease upon the swollen toe,
The ache-contorted finger,
Deceive the frazzled nerve ends into sleep.
Shove off, cockswains, you're loaded.

Here's health to you. I wash you on your way.
Waiting for you to deliver,
I dream of horsebacked statues pale as chalk
Erected to the discoverers of aspirin
Who walk in radiance by the streams of Lethe,
Bayer-assed, in starched hospital dickies.

Sharing the Score

All through *Don Giovanni*, the lovers hold
The cumbersome score between them like a chart
To orchid-spattered islands drenched in storms,
Their fingers pacing to the music's pace,
Limning the legend, skimming note and bar
As, naked, they might trace each other's forms.

Coughs from the curtained boxes, whispered words
Cannot distract this pair from their pursuit
Of paradise. Out of a fast-food bag
They share cold wurst. An orchard brewing fruit,
A paper harp to play glissandi on,
The score ordains the downfall of the Don.

To Mozart's mind, love hallows quenchless thirst.
Turning each page, intent, their fingers glance.
At last Don Pedro's stone shape rumbles in
To ask, "Is dinner ready yet?" Accurst
Hot hands yank Giovanni down to Hell
And passion hurls them off to their hotel.

Daughter Like a Pendant

Beautiful opal on a withered throat,
　　Distraction from a profile now laid waste,
　　The gleam you cast so ignorantly chaste,
Such polish in the study you devote

To mirroring her gestures. Futile scheme,
　　And yet who'd blame her wish that we should see
　　Her slack chin blurred through your transparency?
Her sacrifice: ice milk now, not ice cream,

Reducing wafers, Exercycles, gaunt
　　Mornings in sauna hells—brave tries to stem
　　The sawtoothed nibble of the days. You, gem,
Now are the single beauty she can flaunt.

Uneasily, you boost your bra, forgetting
　　Our surreptitious glances. Straps askew,
　　You giggle at a punchline someone blew.
Already, dear, you loosen in your setting,

Inviting theft. But still, who'd not applaud
　　Her thrust for inattention? You achieve
　　What she desires—before, that is, you leave
And leave your wearer wistful for her gaud.

Pie

Whoever dined in this café before us
Took just a forkful of his cherry pie.
We sit with it between us. Let it lie
Until the overworked waitperson comes
To pick it up and brush away the crumbs.

You look at it. I look at it. I stare
At you. You do not look at me at all.
Somewhere, a crash as unwashed dishes fall.
The clatter of a dropped knife splits the air.
Second-hand smoke infiltrates everywhere.

Your fingers clench the handle of a cup
A stranger drained. I almost catch your eye
For a split second. The abandoned pie
Squats on its plate before us, seeping red
Like a thing not yet altogether dead.

Lyric

Whispering in the wind's wake,
  Young leaves say, riffling
Cheek against trivial cheek,
  What's love? Brief trifling.
Twig spurts, my heart hurts.
  Bloom breeds on bough.
Since cast forth from your arms I can
  Neither stand still nor go.

Now groves of taller trees
  Rouse them to song,
Boughs swaying, ill at ease:
  Little leaves, you are wrong.
Love is long lingering;
  Forgetfulness, slow.
Since cast forth from your arms I can
  Neither stand still nor go.

To His Lover, That She Be Not Overdressed

And why take ye thought for raiment?
—Matthew 6:28

The lilies of the field
   That neither toil nor spin
Stand dazzlingly revealed
   In not a thing but skin

And in that radiant state
   Sheer essences they wear.
Take heed, my fashion plate.
   Be so arrayed. Go bare.

Dusk Decides to Settle in Short Hills

A birdcall snapped off in midair,
   A rain that in descending quit,
A glow the sun can hardly spare
   And village lights that look half-lit

Pierce not quite through. In time to winds,
   Staccato bursts of acorns strafe
Parched dirt. Deliberately, day ends
   The way a broker shuts his safe.

Shriveled Meditation

On junkyard hills the flattened frames
   Of cars that failed to veer
Mount to the sky like damage claims,
   More massive every year.

Long raised, hitchhikers' wistful thumbs
   Lie level with the wind.
Leaves lose their grips. The earth becomes
   Increasingly thick skinned.

State secrets that don't dare survive
   Pour through the greedy shredder
And I and everyone alive
   Go right on growing deader.

Horny Man's Song

When, strolling through the carnival,
I fetch you cotton candy,
Pink sugar clouds stick to your chin.
I feel prodigious randy,
But when at last we come to dine
My high hopes hit the dust—
    If you can't spare me a crumb of love
    Then throw me the crust of lust.

When idling by the baker shop
We smell hot raisin bread,
You just can't stand the risen yeast,
The raw dough's upthrust head.
For one indecent meal I'd die
Or live on, if I must—
    Oh, won't you spare me a crumb of love?
    Then throw me the crust of lust.

Perplexities

We grope for fresh uncertainties by phases,
Lugging our doubts like teddy bears to bed.
When lab rats dream they dream of running mazes.

Psychologists would dissipate our dazes.
They fumble through each couch potato's head.
We grope for fresh uncertainties by phases,

On vexing questions fastening our gazes.
We'd penetrate a shifting wall of lead.
When lab rats dream they dream of running mazes

And desperate for answers suffer crazes.
Delivered by no Ariadne's thread,
We grope for fresh uncertainties by phases.

I'm sick of old perplexities. Sweet Jaysus,
Give us a patch of clarity instead!
When lab rats dream they dream of running mazes.

A moment's clearing—a solution blazes—
But then we're not so sure, and then we're dead.
We grope for fresh uncertainties by phases.
When lab rats dream they dream of running mazes.

Best Intentions

Guilt keeps an attic crammed with things undone,
Old friends ignored, the months-unwritten letter,
Duties we'd sooner shrink from than confront,
But won't let go. Tomorrow we'll do better,
We tell ourselves, and yet remain inert,
Watching our best intentions by the minute
Incubate mildew like a dirty shirt,
An outgrown bassinet, mice nesting in it.

In the Airport Bar

Cooling our heels within this bright
    Pink neon-lit upholstered box,
While, outside, flames deice our flight
    We rattle bourbon on the rocks,
Endure delay and, free from care,
    Consume the day without half trying,
Our thirst for taking to the air
    Quenched by fear of dying.

Ponce de León

Cupped brackish water in his fingers, held
His breath in hope. Attending him, his men
Gaped for the promised miracle, but his skin
Had lost no wrinkle, not one liver spot.
Another false
Fountain that sprang from earth, not from God's garden.

These Everglades
Dissolved men's bones, rusted their cutlass blades.
He felt the night wind harden.
Arthritic raindrops dabbled at his tent.
Was his resolve now, like the wine casks, spent?

Destroying him, the Angel begged his pardon.

Harriet

Bullied by Pound, ran "Prufrock" in the back
Of a dull summer number—shot heard round
The world. Rattling across Siberia
By railcar over tundra, stony ground
Where stunted fir trees struggled to breathe free
Like poets in America, she'd found
Her vision. Stuck out chin—by God, she'd pack
Not pork but poetry.

Vestal, bluestockinged battler—what hard nights
She spent uprooting tick-tock lyricists,
Sowing and weeding fields of neophytes.
Who could have thought the Mountain of the Mists
Would keep her grave when, frail, on Andes heights,
She closed eyes that had blazed like amethysts?

Meditation in the Bedroom of General Francisco Franco

Life is a short night in a bad hotel.
—St. Teresa of Avila

Behind an oak door triple-locked
    And those few soldiers he could trust
To stand with firearm hammers cocked,
    He slept the sweet sleep of the just

While motionless there lay within
    A reliquary by his side
The left hand of Avila's saint,
    In life discalced, now calcified.

How could he think that all his dreams
    Of foes consigned to abrupt rest
By firing squads and torture teams
    Her gracious fingers might have blessed?

What if, one dark night while he slept,
    That hand had stolen from its crypt,
Shedding brown flakes, and softly crept
    Past his mustaches, closely clipped,

Over his lips that faintly hissed,
    Down past each pouch of facial suet
To fasten on his throat and twist?
    Teresa, you had your chance. You blew it.

A Mobile

Blowing sets them going,
These thin tin things
Hung on hairsprings:
Poised as in a daze they dull,
Blaze, dim, and turn
Only to return
To their own mirrors to be beautiful.
See how they wave, impaled
On strands of light that rise,
Tilting their heads to quavers of the air,
Blundering downward: sun-stunned butterflies.

Now drawn
Into entanglements they move, a lawn-
Party that each plate
Has to circumnavigate,
Conversing. Now a hand
Sweeps in a casual gesture of command,
Then, of fresh mind,
Dismisses weight and flings
Aside earth in an instant of despair,
Leaving the daylight glinting on its rings.

Small fry circle a shark shape, warily
Keeping their distances from any lunge—
Then the whole school revolves
In panic hunger, swarms,
Defining what its orbit so informs:
That strengths are set at ease and weaknesses
Held momentarily
Under enough stress.

Christmas Show at the Planetarium

Under a dome of stainless steel
    A robot locust's twin cloned brains
Revolve their beams. The houselights dull,
    A voice vast as the Lord's complains:

"What mighty light burst from the east?
    Was it, astronomers suppose,
Some worn-out dwarf star that increased
    In prominence in its dying throes?

"Or did two planets, by chance sent
    Down nearby tracks (some have suspected)
To simple shepherd eyes look blent
    As on their rounds they intersected?"

Somehow, beneath sheet-metal skies,
    No wonder glows, no urge to kneel.
Projected constellations wheel.
    What would we see if we were wise?

Maples in January

for Edgar Bowers

By gust and gale brought down to this
  Simplicity, they stand unleaved
  And momentarily reprieved
From preening photosynthesis.

Abandoned, tons of greenery.
  As though scorched bare by forest fire,
  They've shrugged the rustle of desire,
The chore of being scenery,

And now impervious to thirst,
  No longer thrall to summer's sway,
  They stand their ground as if to say,
Winter and wind, come do your worst.

In Defense of New England

Having to do without spring
 Is New Englanders' annual dues:
Buds jerk open, late robins sing
 Quick choruses, peepers refuse

To chirp more than two or three days.
 From the maple trunk, sap trickles thin
And drunken with heat, in a daze,
 Drab summer comes staggering in.

Some years the one portent we know
 That winter's begun to unravel
Is when, through the fraying-out snow,
 Kids' sled runners knock sparks from gravel.

I hear there are spots on the globe
 Where the same season lasts for all time,
Where the light's as incessant as strobe,
 And admitting you're bored is high crime.

Obdurate Snow

Crusted with oil and soot,
Crags of the last snowfall of March refuse
To go away though crocuses break sod.
They sun themselves like snoozing walruses.

No use to prod with shovel, pick, or shoe
Their twice-refrozen icecaps. Taken root,
They hunker down, determined to endure
Every humiliation
As though convinced that winter is for sure
And any thaw a moment's aberration.

Pacifier

her night thoughts

My baby wails. That I may rest
I offer him a rubber breast
And soon as waves by oil suppressed,

He quiets. An underhanded trick
Yet practical and politic—
He cries for bread, I give him brick,

But when night circles round to four
I open to him like a door
And yield him all he wants and more.

As old wives say, it may be true
That love too frequent can undo.
Sometimes give just the likes of you.

Your lover's tide may rise in flood
When there's no answer in your blood.
Then let that raging bull chew cud

And go to sleep. Let him return
When in coincidence you burn.
Fire lingers near a kindled urn

And lives to burn again and spreads
On real as on imagined beds
Held fast by things that stand in steads.

September Twelfth, 2001

Two caught on film who hurtle
from the eighty-second floor,
choosing between a fireball
and to jump holding hands,

aren't us. I wake beside you,
stretch, scratch, taste the air,
the incredible joy of coffee
and the morning light.

Alive, we open eyelids
on our pitiful share of time,
we bubbles rising and bursting
in a boiling pot.

Notes

The bulk of this collection is work done in the past decade, but two or three items were begun much earlier. There are also six, first printed before 1991, that I had not wanted to collect without giving them a final scrub.

NAOMI TRIMMER.   This is a true story; even the unlikely name is real. In the 1930s in Dover, New Jersey, Miss Trimmer was one of several harmless lunatics who freely walked the streets, inspiring amusement and affection. That she had lost her mind as a result of her traumatic concert début was one legend surrounding her. Another was that her father had offered a large cash reward to any man who would marry her, but had found no takers.

THE BALLAD OF FENIMORE WOOLSON AND HENRY JAMES. That a subtle history has been crudely simplified is a fair charge against this ballad, all the truer if it is read as strict biography. I have invented certain details (such as Fenimore's forwardness at the Hyde Park riots), omitted others (such as James's second stay in Florence under her roof). The main events are drawn from Leon Edel's account in *Henry James*, volumes 2 and 3. Cheryl B. Tornsey, in *Constance Fenimore Woolson: The Grief of Artistry* (1989), suggests that the critically praised and financially successful Woolson suffered from depression, not from unrequited love. Whatever the truth, it seems clear that James, in shocked reaction to her suicide, believed that he might have prevented it. Stanzas 11–13 echo Woolson's letter from Florence in 1880: her first impressions of James. In fact, six years elapsed between that letter and James's first stay in her Florentine villa. Stanza 20 is based on a journal entry Woolson made shortly before her death. Both documents are given by Clare Benedict in *Constance Fenimore Woolson* (1930). Stanza 31 draws from James's letter of 1907, following his last visit to Woolson's grave.

OBSCENITY.   Oyster Nan, a lusty Billingsgate vendor who openly demands gratification, figures in the popular song "As Oyster Nan stood by her tub," collected by Thomas D'Urfey in *Wit and Mirth; or, Pills to Purge Melancholy*, volume 5 (1719–20).

BALLADE OF THE HANGED.   This is a version of the "Ballade des Pendus," sometimes called "L'Epitaphe Villon." Villon wrote this poem in 1463, when, charged with taking part in a brawl that injured a lawyer, he was sentenced to be "hanged and strangled." After his successful appeal, his sentence was commuted to banishment.

Acknowledgments

"A Beard of Bees" first appeared in The Atlantic Monthly; "Then and Now," in Blue Unicorn; "Five-and-Dime, Late Thirties," in Boulevard; "Taking Aspirin," in Carolina Quarterly; "Obdurate Snow," in The Christian Science Monitor; "Best Intentions," in Chronicles; "Christmas Show at the Planetarium," in Cumberland Poetry Review; "Décor" and "Pie," in The Dark Horse (Scotland); "Street Moths" and "To His Lover, That She Be Not Overdressed," in Defined Providence; "Afterward" (later version), in Eclectic Literary Forum; "In Defense of New England," in The Edge City Review; "Epitaph Proposed for the Headstone of S. R. Quiett" and "A Scandal in the Suburbs," in The Epigrammatist; "Pileup," in Four Quarters; "In the Airport Bar" and "On Song," in Gulf Coast; "A Curse on a Thief," in Harvard Review; "The Ballad of Fenimore Woolson and Henry James," "Close Call," and "Meditation in the Bedroom of General Francisco Franco," in Hudson Review (vol. 46, no. 2, summer 1993, and vol. 54, no. 2, summer 2001); "The Homeless in Cairo Cemetery," "Thebes: In the Robber Village," and "Visit," in Image: A Journal of the Arts & Religion; "Daughter Like a Pendant," in Iowa Review; "Ballade of the Hanged," in Janus; "Dusk Decides to Settle in Short Hills" and "Horny Man's Song," in Journal of New Jersey Poets; "Maples in January," in La Fontana; "Covering the Massacre," in Margie: The American Journal of Poetry; "Police Court Saturday Morning" and "The Spoke," in Medicinal Purposes; "Ponce de León," in New CollAge; "Sharing the Score," in The New Criterion; "Terminals," in The New Statesman; "Shriveled Meditation," in The North Stone Review; "Mustafa Ferrari" and "Obscenity," in Paintbrush; "Commuter," in Piedmont Review; "Others," in Pivot; "For Allen Ginsberg," "Harriet," and "The Purpose of Time Is to Prevent Everything from Happening at Once," in Poetry; "A Mobile," in Princeton University Library Chronicle; "Perplexities," in Rattapallax; "Afterward" (earlier version), in Reck; "Miss Olive Leahy's Rooms & Cigar Divan," in The

Review; "Deer Ticks," in *Rosebud*; "Jimmy Harlow" and "Sailors with the Clap," in *The Sewanee Review* (vol. 109, no. 1, winter 2001); "Naomi Trimmer," in *Sewanee Theological Review*; "Invocation" and "In the Holding Lounge at Frankfurt Airport," in *Smartish Pace*; "Pacifier," in *South Coast Poetry Journal*; "Heard through the Walls of the Racetrack Glen Motel," "Lyric," and "A Snapshot Rediscovered," in *Southern California Anthology*; "Mr. Longfellow's Iron Pen," in *Sou'wester*; "Salute Sweet Deceptions," in *Spirit*; and "The Blessing of the Bikes," in *Texas Review*.

"A Curse on a Thief" appeared in *The Best American Poetry, 1999*, ed. Robert Bly (New York: Scribner, 1999).

"For Allen Ginsberg" appeared in *Literature for Composition*, sixth edition, ed. Sylvan Barnet, Morton Berman, William Burto, William E. Cain, and Marcia Stubbs (New York: Longman, 2002); and in "*And What Rough Beast: Poems at the End of the Century*," ed. Robert McGovern and Stephen Haven (Ashland, Ohio: Ashland Poetry Press, 1999).

"A Scandal in the Suburbs" appeared in *Divine Inspiration: The Life of Jesus in World Poetry*, ed. Robert Atwan, George Dardess, and Peggy Rosenthal (New York: Oxford University Press, 1998).

"September Twelfth, 2001" first appeared in the anthology *September 11, 2001*, ed. William Heyen (Silver Spring, Md.: Etruscan Press, 2002).

"Pacifier" and "Pileup" appeared in a chapbook, *Winter Thunder* (Florence, Ky.: Robert L. Barth, 1990).

"Jimmy Harlow" was published as a one-poem pamphlet (Anchorage, Alaska: Salmon Run Press, 1994).

Six of these poems appeared in a limited edition, *The Purpose of Time* (West Chester, Pa.: Aralia Press, 2002).